A Cat and a Hat

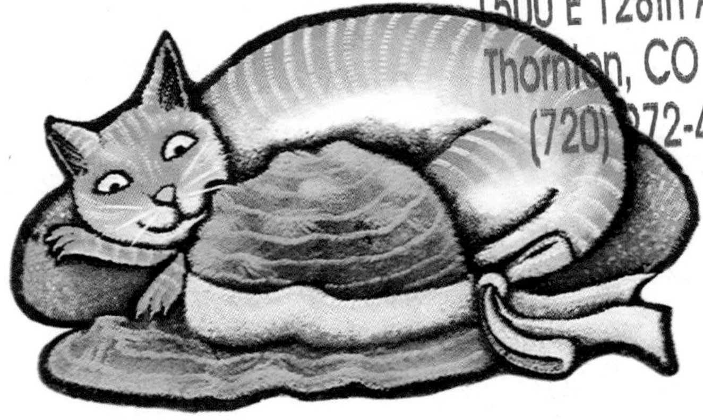

Written by Elizabeth Apgar
Illustrated by Robert Bender

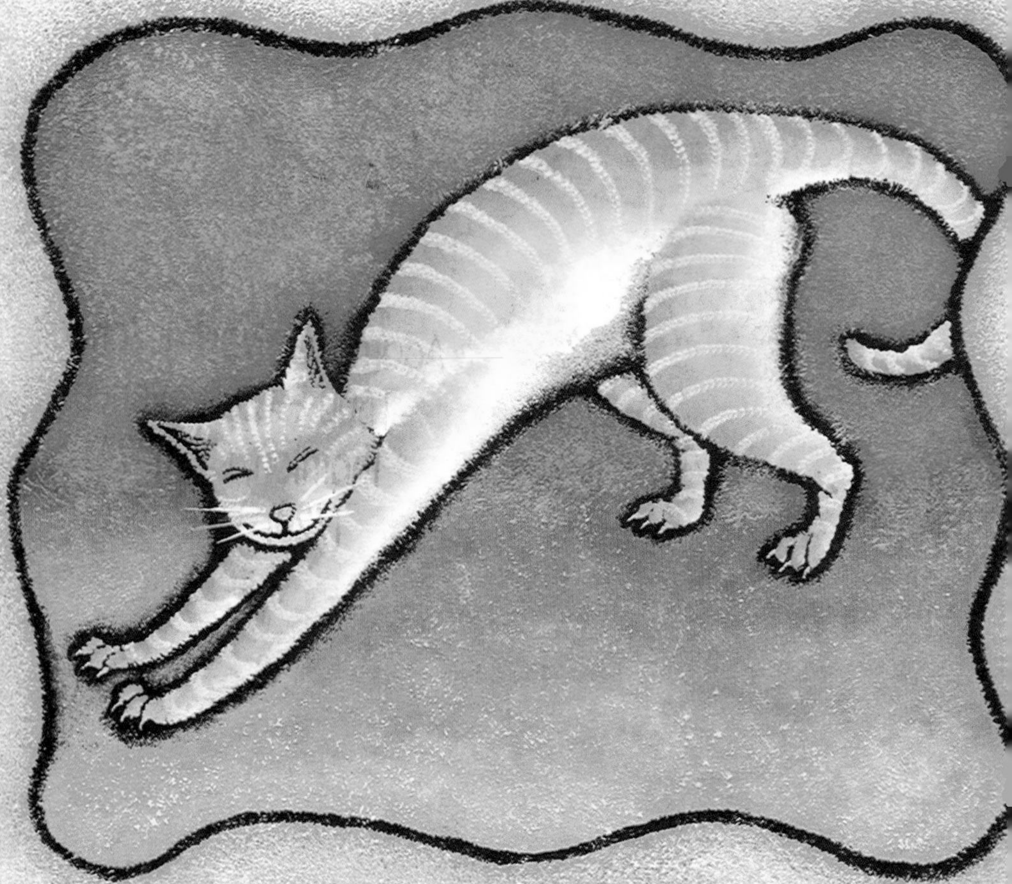

A cat.

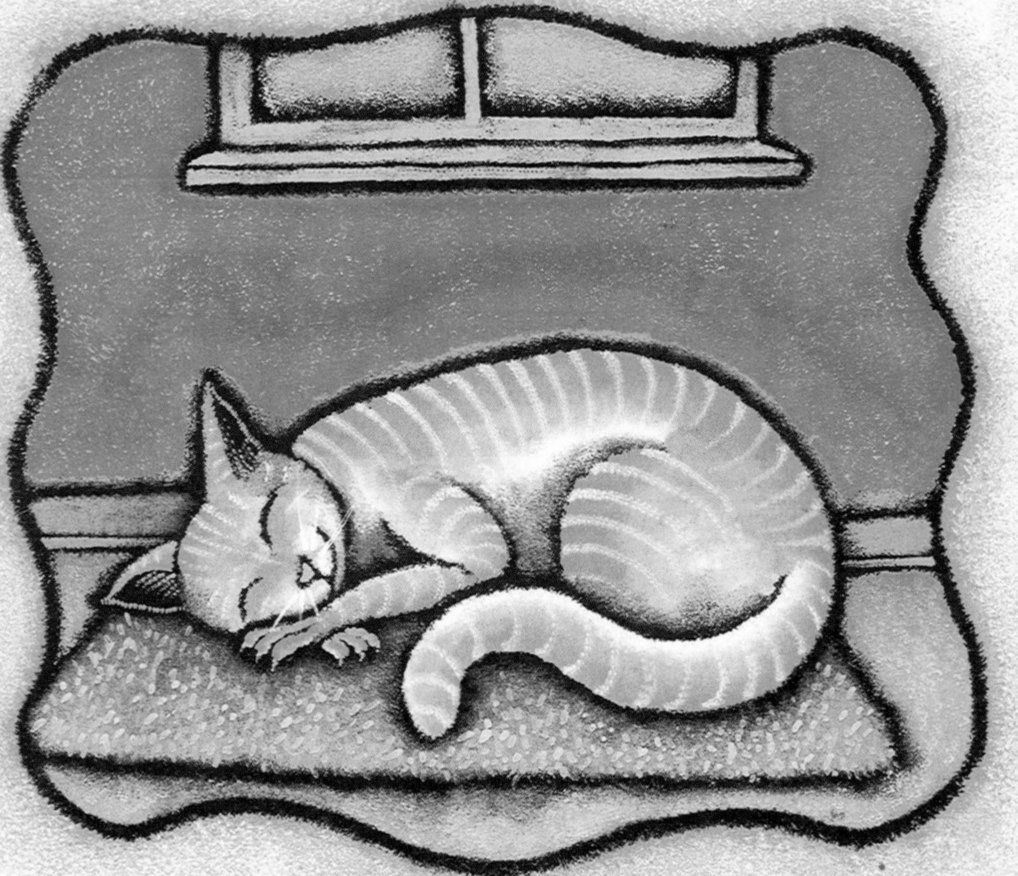

A cat and a mat.

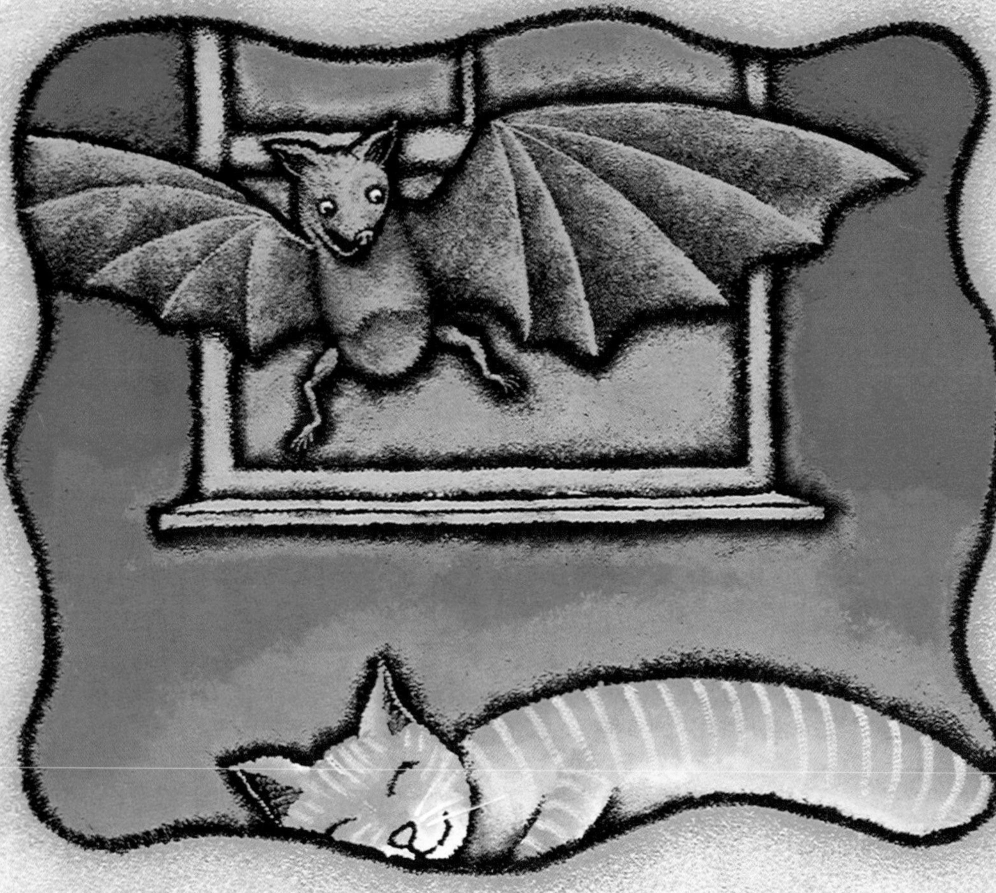

A bat.

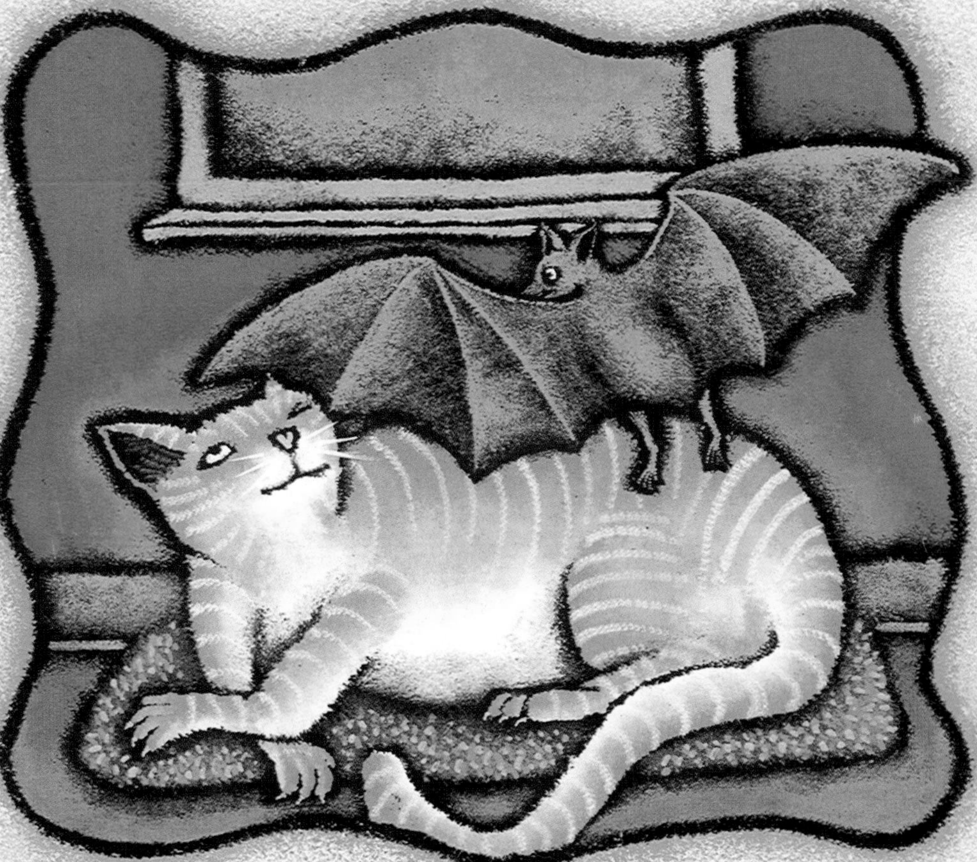

A cat and a bat.

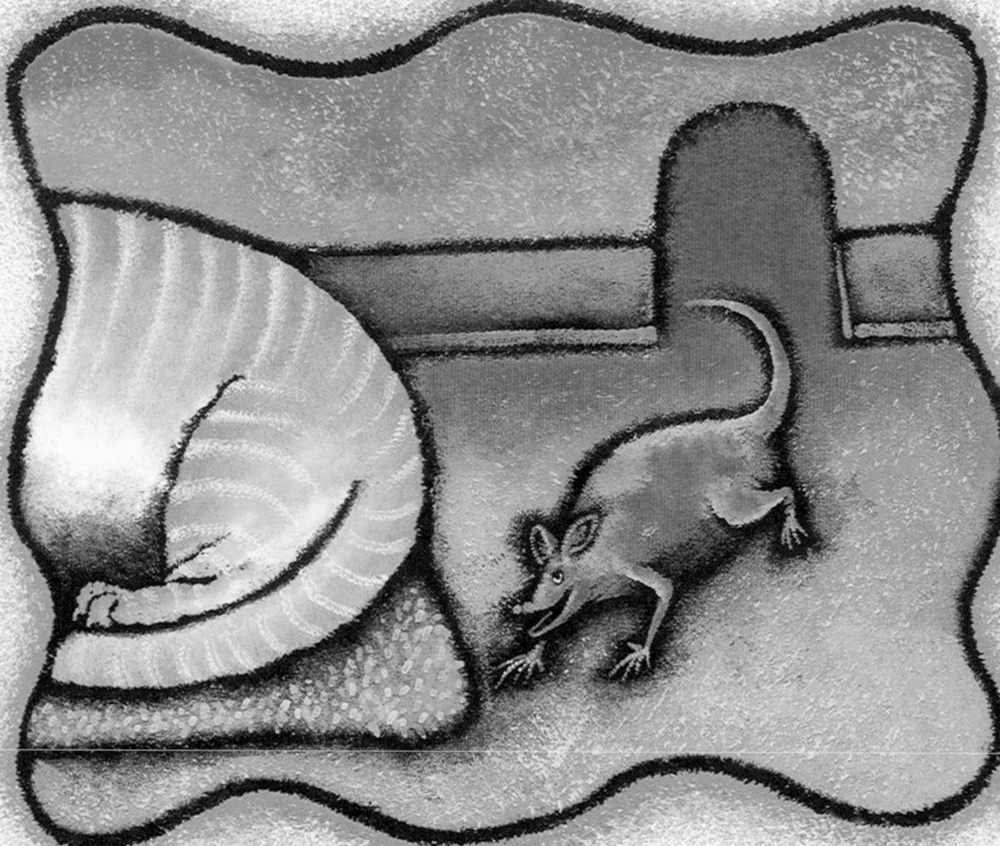

A rat.

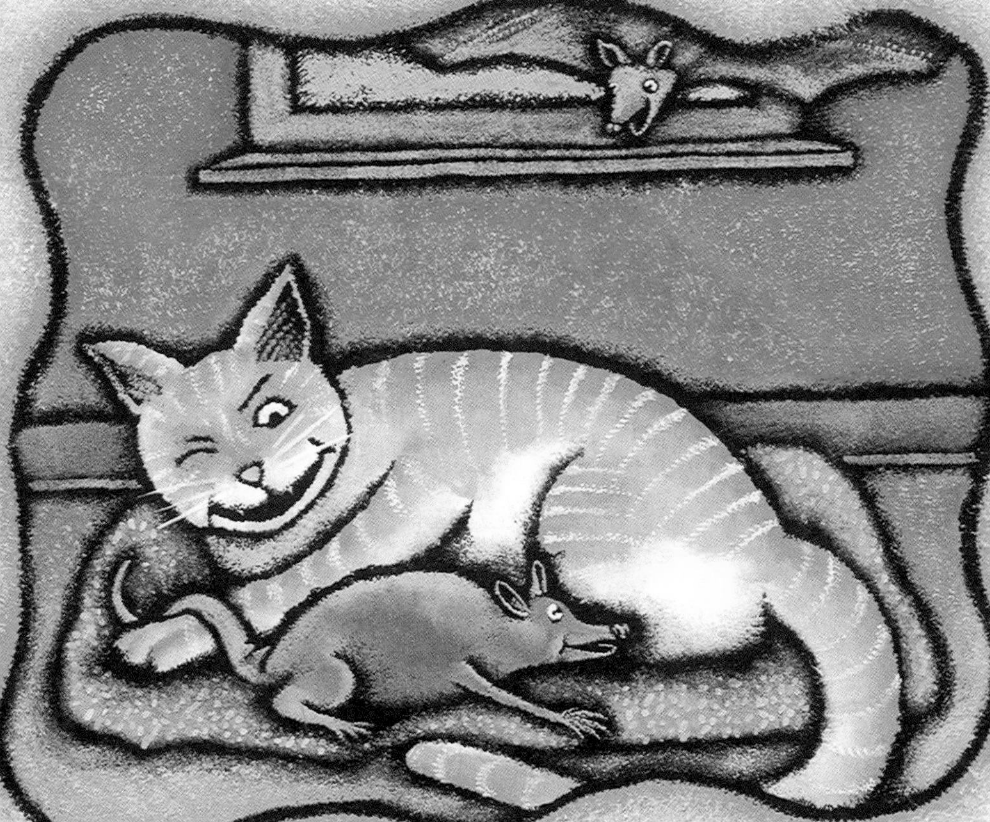

A cat and a rat.

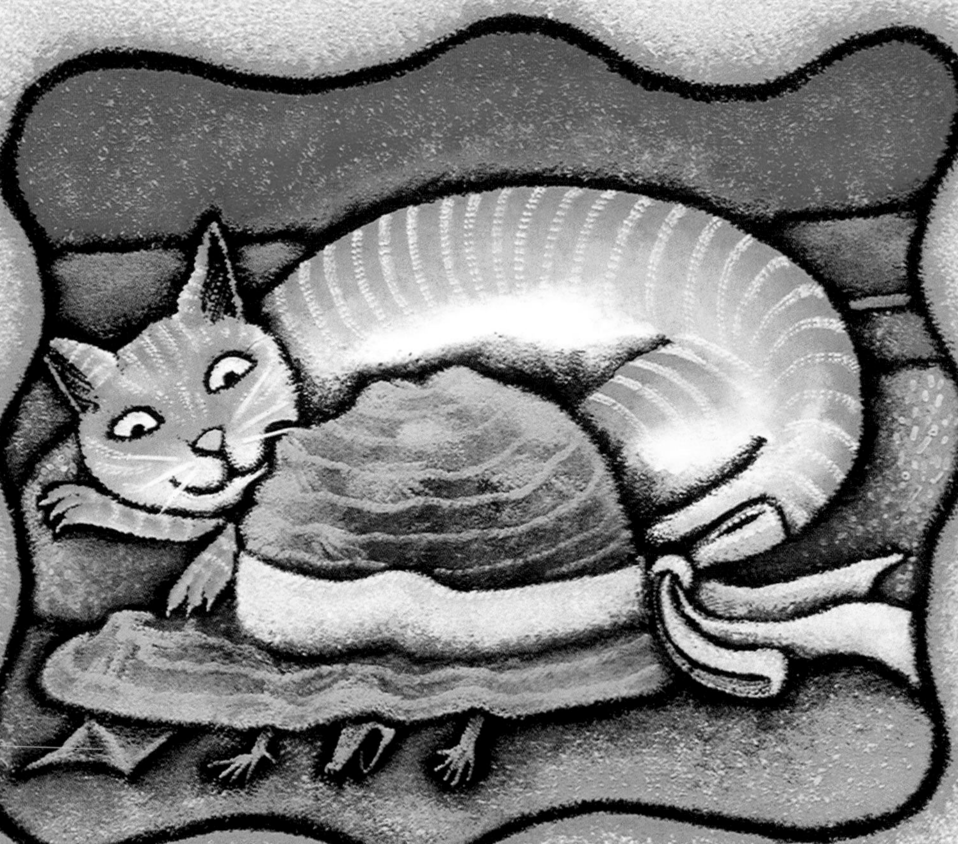

A cat and a hat!